CULTURES CONNECT US!

TRADITIONS

BY AGATHA GREGSON

Gareth Stevens
PUBLISHING

Please visit our website, www.garethstevens.com. For a free color catalog of all our high-quality books, call toll free 1-800-542-2595 or fax 1-877-542-2596.

Library of Congress Cataloging-in-Publication Data

Names: Gregson, Agatha, author.
Title: Traditions / Agatha Gregson.
Description: New York : Gareth Stevens Publishing, 2020. | Series: Cultures connect us! | Includes index.
Identifiers: LCCN 2018042002| ISBN 9781538238547 (pbk.) | ISBN 9781538238561 (library bound) | ISBN 9781538238554 (6-pack)
Subjects: LCSH: Manners and customs–Juvenile literature.
Classification: LCC GT85 .G74 2020 | DDC 395–dc23
LC record available at https://lccn.loc.gov/2018042002

Published in 2020 by
Gareth Stevens Publishing
111 East 14th Street, Suite 349
New York, NY 10003

Designer: Reann Nye
Editor: Therese Shea

Photo credits: series art (background) Lukasz Szwaj/Shutterstock.com; cover Dee Browning/Shutterstock.com; p. 5 Monkey Business Images/Shutterstock.com; p. 7 Oleksandr Fediuk/Shutterstock.com; p. 9 https://commons.wikimedia.org/ wiki/File:M%C3%A5rten_Eskil_Winge_-_Tor%27s_Fight_with_the_Giants_-_Google_ Art_Project.jpg; p. 11 Bettmann/Getty Images; p. 13 Nikhil Patil/iStock / Getty Images Plus/Getty Images; p. 15 subman/E+/Getty Images; p. 17 Zhang Peng/LightRocket/ Getty Images; p. 19 Jeremy Woodhouse/Blend Images/Getty Images; p. 21 Zurijeta/ Shutterstock.com.

Printed in the United States of America

CPSIA compliance information: Batch #CS19GS: For further information contact Gareth Stevens, New York, New York at 1-800-542-2595.

CONTENTS

Boldface words appear in the glossary.

Connecting a Community

Traditions are stories, beliefs, and ways of life passed from **generation** to generation. Going to a Fourth of July parade every year is a tradition. So is putting teeth under a pillow for a tooth fairy! Traditions are an important part of communities.

Every **culture** has traditions. Traditions help connect people to their culture and to each other. They help people remember ideas, values, and history that are important to the culture. It's useful to look closely at traditions to learn what they really mean!

Oral Tradition

Before writing, **information** was passed on by word of mouth. This is called the oral tradition. Some information was in the form of myths. These **fictional** stories pass on ideas about why things happen. Thor is the god who makes thunder in **Norse** myths.

Legends are traditional stories with some truth. For example, Davy Crockett was a real person, but he probably didn't kill a bear when he was 3 years old! Oral tradition also passed on a culture's history and even its laws.

Traditional Dress

Clothes can also be cultural traditions. Many women in India wear a sari, a kind of wrapped dress that has been worn for thousands of years. In Japan, most people wear western-style clothing, but traditional kimonos are worn on special **occasions**.

sari

13

The Xhosa women of Africa have been wrapping their heads in colorful **fabric** for over 400 years. Scots have been wearing **kilts** since the 1500s. Beads have been an important part of Native American dress for thousands of years!

Traditional Music

Many cultures around the world pass on music as part of their traditions. Some Christmas carols, or songs, you may know have been sung since the 1800s. Kun Qu (KWIN CHU) **opera** has been performed in China since the 1300s!

The traditional Mexican music called mariachi began in the late 1700s or early 1800s. Both the clothing styles and the **instruments** of mariachi bands have changed since then. Women are mariachi musicians now, too. Traditions can change over time as cultures change.

Traditional Foods

Food is important to every culture. Communities often gather for meals. Can you think of a traditional dish in your family? Ask an adult to help you make it. Then, ask friends to help you eat it. Traditions should be shared!

GLOSSARY

culture: a group of people with certain beliefs and ways of life

fabric: a kind of cloth

fictional: made up

generation: a group of people born about the same time

information: knowledge obtained from study or observation

instrument: an object used to make music

kilt: a type of skirt traditionally worn by men in Scotland

Norse: relating to ancient Norway

occasion: a special event or time

opera: a play that is sung to music

FOR MORE INFORMATION

BOOKS

Aloian, Molly. *Cultural Traditions in South Africa*. New York, NY: Crabtree Publishing Company, 2014.

Frisch, Aaron. *The History and Traditions of Christmas*. Mankato, MN: RiverStream, 2014.

Ingalls, Ann. *Birthday Traditions Around the World*. Mankato, MN: The Child's World, 2013.

WEBSITES

Explore the World
kids.nationalgeographic.com/world/
Pick a country on the map and explore!

Traditions Change Over Time
www.iptv.org/iowapathways/mypath/traditions-change-over-time
Read about different traditions and how they've changed.

INDEX